Songs of the Ancestral Home

Dedication

For my late parents,
Anna F. H. van Dÿken-Hidding
and Heiko van Dÿken.

The late Roelof (Roy) Kippers
and Reinier Kippers,
our second son.
25 October, 1948 - 4 January, 1949

Songs of the Ancestral Home

Poems by

Hendrien Kippers

With a Foreword by Doris Calder

Chapel Street Editions
Woodstock, New Brunswick

Published by Chapel Street Editions,
Woodstock, NB, Canada
www.chapelstreeteditions.com

Library and Archives Canada Cataloguing in Publication

Kippers, Hendrien, author

Songs of the ancestral home : poems by Hendrien Kippers / with a foreword by Doris Calder.

ISBN 978-0-9936725-1-4 (pbk.)

I. Title.

PS8571.I6325S66 2014 C811'.54 C2014-905220-0

Designed by Helmuth Productions using Adobe® InDesign.®
The typeface used is Adobe Caslon Pro. Designed by Carol Twombly, Adobe Caslon Pro is a revival of Caslon, based on William Caslon's original specimen pages printed between 1734 and 1770.

Cover illustration: "Sunny Acres" - a needlepoint by Mary Jane Kippers.

Sunny Acres is the name Hendrien Kippers gave to the Hampton Road homestead in Quispamsis, New Brunswick where she and her family lived for many years. Her daughter, Mary Jane, created this needlepoint tableau of house, trees and workshop on Dutch linen while visiting the Netherlands. The opening suite of poems, "The Ancestral Home," was written about this house at Sunny Acres.

Photograph of the author by Brendan Helmuth

Contents

Acknowledgments

There are many people I would like to thank for making this book possible.

First of all my teachers: the late Kay Smith, Dr. Anne Compton, and Phyllis Rowan who gave me a skein of blue yarn for an object poem.

My friends at the "Poetry Group Without a Name" - Mary Lou Joyce, our hostess with her delicious treats, her husband Bill, Betty Thompkins for getting me there, and all the other participants for keeping me writing and interested.

Keith Helmuth sorted my poems by topics and so made order in my wandering mind and suggested the title.

My best friend Doris Calder provided editing assistance, careful attention to the preparation of the final manuscript, and wrote the Foreword.

My friend Rob Roy put the poems on a disc so they could be sent to Keith and Brendan Helmuth, the publishers at Chapel Street Editions. Brendan Helmuth designed this attractive book and brought it into print. Thanks to you all!

Foreword

Hendrien Van Dijken was born in Groningen, the Netherlands in 1928, the third of four children. From 1940 to 1945 she lived under the Nazi occupation, during which her parents were active in the Dutch resistance movement. As for so many others during those years, anxiety, uprootedness, and deprivation were chronic realities for her and her family. The impact of these wartime experiences surely contributed to her sense of longing for a home that was safe.

In 1946 she married Roelof Kippers, and in 1948 she and their baby Ernst joined him in what was then the Dutch East Indies. Roelof had gone on ahead to work on patrol boats of the Dutch East Indian Coast Guard. In 1951 they immigrated to Canada, living for several years in Ontario. In 1960 they came to New Brunswick and moved into the old farmhouse central to the poems in Part I of this book. Hendrien Kippers lived in this farm house for 35 years leading a very busy life as the mother of ten children. At the same time she did volunteer work in the community, kept informed on local and world events, and cared deeply about issues of peace and justice. It was many years before she was able to expand her life with academic studies, but in time she did and was awarded a B.A. in English Literature. Her deep appreciation for the visual arts often took her to the Saint John Arts Centre where she became a volunteer. She has long been a faithful supporter of local art and crafts, as well as being an enthusiastic participant in local writing and poetry groups.

Songs of the Ancestral Home represents one of the longest continuing literary forms, the poetics of place. Writers of such literature are often inspired by their deep attachment and love for the place where they live. They "belong" to a particular place which can be felt by them to include many aspects - the land, the people, the rhythms of nature and the rhythms of life itself. We feel this attachment strongly in the poetry of Hendrien Kippers. Her poems help us to appreciate the ancestral home that each one of us has. Some of us are perhaps deeply connected to a family homestead or to a particular city, town or village. Others may not be. However, we each have an inextricable connection to our common ancestral home - Earth. We are connected to Earth and to the whole community of life on many levels. These poems gently remind us of this, as the poet paints a living picture, not only of the old farmhouse, but also of her wider home, the city of Saint John with its natural features so powerfully impacted by the Bay of Fundy.

Throughout this collection, by direct observation, reflection and metaphor, the poet conveys the importance of ongoing generational connection and one's place in it. We also feel her experiences of struggle and pain, of coping with inner turmoil and grief. Yet the last section of the book resounds with joy and liberation. We sense the healing which can come from a deep association with the natural world, from an appreciation of culture, and from the love of family and friends.

Songs of the Ancestral Home is composed of six sections. In part one, the old farmhouse itself, as well as several of its features, speaks directly to us. It begins with the words: "I am old beyond knowing." The spirit of the house then takes us back to its beginnings and leads us through the passage of time and life in that place:

Hand-made nails and hand-hewn beams...,
candle lights and smoky oil lamps to magic electricity.

Each room, a door, a window, a hallway, converses as a living presence.

The *Parlour* speaks:

I've rejoiced in sing-songs at
family gatherings, listened to soul talks with pastor and priest...

And the *Wood Stove* declares:

I am Hestia – hearth, focus of home and household,
nourishing bodies and nourishing souls...

And the author, who herself spent decades around the hearth in that farmhouse, nourishing bodies and nourishing souls, speaks authentically of "simmering stews", "baking bread", "burning wood", "festive dinners", and "chatty farewells".

The *Master Bedroom* speaks with a poignancy readily understood by anyone who has lived in a home where generations have left their mark, both seen and unseen:

First cry, last sigh;
these are my epiphanies:
Too often they became one.

In part two we realize how intricately the city of Saint John and the Bay of Fundy are linked. Old Saint John, home to the ancestors of countless people, was founded and developed because of the existence of the bay. Fundy's tides, its "mighty roar", sculpted the landscape and brought the people to it's shores... "loyal subjects... eager market merchants and ferrying fishing fleet...". And always there are the gulls, screaming and "tracing arches from bay to shore...".

Hendrien Kippers realizes her ancestral Earth connection, as we can see in *Slack Tide Surprise*:

> *When I stepped out to greet the Bay as usual,*
> *I knew she would be there, as always she had been,*
> *Eons before I knew her.*

The poems are filled with colours, sounds, smells, and with fresh, appealing imagery as in *Spring Fever*:

> *The Bay is skittish this morning-*
> *like a racehorse too long waiting...*

We can share the author's pleasure in an uptown gallery hop, a Sunday morning stroll along Harbour Passage, or feel the "Polar cold on the Harbour Bridge" as she waits impatiently for millennium fireworks and the countdown to midnight. Sometimes her imagery almost transforms a poem into an oil painting, while at the same time incorporating movement into the still life:

> *Greying sky surrounds the falling*
> *Sun; curling waves encouraged*
> *By the sea wind, separate the granite*
> *Bay from the silvery beach*
> *Prior to the darkness of night.*

And always, the close connection between the Bay and the City:

The roar
came with me
when I left the Bay.

In part three we read:

It was the trees that grabbed my soul.

This opening line of *Soul Grabbers* grabs us, as it expresses the powerful effect the trees had upon the poet as she was searching for a place to put down *her* roots. The tall, stately trees are such a strong presence that they "captured" her into making their ancestral home hers. She sees them

placed in a graceful curve, sentinels
filled with stories
of many lives, of times long past.

She identifies with them and what they symbolize.

The poems in this section all express Hendrien Kippers' deep communion with nature, whether it is her whimsical observations of migrating wild geese, her sober thoughts about an oak leaf in *Last Survivor*:

twirling like a whirligig,
fighting a force fierce enough
to topple trees

or a graphic description of a dead crow lying in the gutter:

Neatly on her back,
wings and feet folded,
prim and ready as if
waiting for an open casket...

In this short, evocative poem, *Dead Crow*, we feel a tangible sense of grief over the crow's demise, and realize that all creatures have innate worth and dignity.

Part four begins with a short series of poems based on the author's childhood memories of the Netherlands. Four of the poems deal directly with her experiences of war. *Herfte, The Netherlands, May 10, 1940* is written as she remembered it - a real life drama. We feel the intensity, shock, and apprehension when her family finds out the German army is invading their town. It is a critical moment full of uncertainty and impending doom. Their ancestral home, the Netherlands, is about to become a place of great travail, the effects of which will continue for generations.

The poems in this section are the most poignant of all. Although written from a place of much soul searching and deep personal suffering, there is no trace of self-pity. Instead, they convey a universal resonance. Here the author is pouring out her soul with discipline and care, a necessary part of healing. Bravely confronting the "mountains", the "mudslides", "cave-ins and torrents", at last she knows, "...I moved mountains that had to be moved." Again, she finds strength and release in nature. In the poem *Liberation* she identifies with:

One gull, single keeper of the sky,
Testing her mettle
Against the storm
Setting me free.

Part five is composed as a series of portraits not just of people, but also of ordinary, commonplace things. We see Hendrien Kippers' gift of observing something and then taking it from the practical to the philosophical, as in *A Box Full of Questions*. Here she speculates on the life of an unknown person in a foreign land who handcrafted a souvenir box she finds for sale in Saint John.

In *Bread I* and *Bread II* she reflects on this primary food in both positive and negative ways. In *Bread I* she writes:

To satisfy an honest hunger earned
Through forthright work, and blessings at the table.

In *Bread II* her thoughts take a darker turn:

Give us this day our daily bread has now
become an order rather than a plea.
Where nature once was Queen and led the plough,
We now have progress King and ethics flee...
Not needs, but greed in charge and forcing yields...
While bread as symbol lost it worth
And work its pride, we smothered Mother Earth.

In a *Skein of Wool* she focuses on a simple skein to reflect on the generational theme:

a thread connecting generations
far back into antiquity
and reaching forward
tentatively
not sure about its destination.

Part six sings of blessings and joy in life. This set of poems expresses gratitude for the warmth of the morning sun, for a visit from a tiny yellow spider, for rainbows, for the presence of two companions, Wind and Rain, who accompanied her on an otherwise solitary walk, sharing:

their strength to pit my strength against...
their play to stimulate my joy...
their energy so I could feel my own.

The poems in this last section illustrate the fulfillment to be found from courageously and enthusiastically embracing life:

All the things I want to do,
to see, to hear, to learn...
Do I try to do too much? Want too much?
No, not at all! In spite of all these little irritations...
I still had a great day!

There is gratitude, too, for continuing generations, as expressed in *Three Roses*:

...three roses for me–
one for Hendrien,
one for mother,

one for oma.
Three in one,
each completing me.

The poems in *Songs of the Ancestral Home* show us that whatever comes to us in life, whatever struggles and pain shake our foundations, there is still joy to be found and experienced when we can live with a sense of wonder and belonging in our "ancestral home". The following lines, written while traveling in the high desert of the American Southwest, are a testament to the author's ultimate faith in the beauty and grandeur of life, and the importance of her integral part in it.

I feel so inconsequential, so small, so finite
In this vast expanse of sky and land,
Yet also know that all would not be as is
Without my being here,
An integral part of this infinite, awesome expanse of love,
Its human input blending as natural as that of other life;
Timeless, yet acute, structured in its formlessness,
A place where God rests on the seventh day.

Doris Calder
Long Reach, New Brunswick
April, 2014

Doris Calder is the author of *All Our Born Days: A Lively History of New Brunswick's Kingston Peninsula.* She was associated with the founding of the St. John River Society and was instrumental in the making of the documentary film, *The Lower Saint John: A Gift of River.*

Songs of the Ancestral Home

PROLOGUE

I am old beyond knowing.

Built in times of simple craftsmanship,
muscle power, basic needs and
neighbourly co-operation, I became a house.
With sturdy walls, a shingled roof,
birch bark insulation,
handmade nails and hand-hewn beams, small windows all around
and gingerbread to add a whimsical, personal touch;
thus I came into being.

Then – folks made this house a home.

An old primary path, trod down by native peoples,
snaked by the front door,
later to be overshadowed by handsome elms,
which kept the cold north winds at bay,
sheltering countless generations of birds,
squirrels and other creatures and
providing arms to hang children's swings.

The land, stretching from lake far into the woods, and
with steady labour kept
human needs fulfilled.
Apple trees were planted and later
lilacs to fill a fancier urge.

Time brought changes;
the needs of people shift.
A new road, now straight from town to town,
saved time for travelers and left a circular drive,
granting privacy to people living here.

My interior adjusted to changing needs and wants.
Walls were moved, taken out, replaced and,
like many an aging girth, my size expanded.

From candle lights and smoky oil lamps to
magic electricity:
From drudgy bucket-well to outside hand-pump, then,
inside plumbing:
From dusty wood stoves to central heating:
Each change a chance
to free human energy and minds for
more leisure and expanded vision.
From local gossip and concerns
to worldwide interaction.

I've seen generations come and go;
deals for my sale by handshake replaced
by big "For Sale" signs.
Nevertheless, I feel the end approaching,
a time I will be no more.
Even so, I feel at peace.

Folks made my space a home.

I sheltered many a generation,
gave comfort, asylum, rest,
and feel appreciated for it all.

I have been loved.

FRONT DOOR

Janus-like, I face in two directions, but
with a different focus;
one inward, the other out to the wide beyond.

I am hinged to help or hinder
crossing to the other side.

I am the portal of importance – the way to the parlour.

Travellers who traverse my threshold
are few, and not the ordinary kind;
unanticipated strangers, turned collars,
guests to celebrations or wakes, and
corpses, feet first.

Mostly, I am in repose,
firmly closed, watching,
holding back the elements and the unwanted,
secure in my place.

Parlour

Used least, I command the greatest care.
Convention rules, still, each mistress
played with my limits in a creativity
not warranted elsewhere.
Rich wallpaper, ordered from Boston,
images of stern ancestors stared down on all who entered,
pianos or organs graced my walls,
dark velvet draped my windows and,
when "hydro" came, a pleasing chandelier
added style to the ceiling.
A fireplace was built with sturdy store-bought bricks.
Floors of painted pine boards,
later overlaid with shining oak,
and cushioned with braided rugs.
Furnishings were sparse but carefully chosen
for looks, not comfort.

Yet all this dress is just one facet of the many
that rule the human heart:
Another – my function – deals with life itself, the
celebration of baptism, marriage and wake –
joyful welcome and sad farewell;
I shared in all.

I've rejoiced in the sing-songs at family gatherings,
listened to soul-talks with pastor and priest,
seen masks cover "unacceptable" feelings and
new romances chaperoned duly (with envy or joy) –
all moments of import, preserving pride and
prejudice.

DINING ROOM

In daily life I am a stand-by,
my table contracted, lace cloth and centerpiece in repose.
Chairs primly lined along the walls
like pickling jars.
The sideboard is bare, save for the empty bowls and platters,
passed on through generations,
acquiring cracks and chips with stories all their own.

Come feast-days though, I am the center,
receiving the crown of what went on in the kitchen for days.
The table, now stretched to full capacity, is loaded with
a centerpiece of turkey or ham, temptingly spreading delicious aroma,
surrounded by ample mainstays and savoury condiments –
the bounty of women's skills and care, Epicurean-led.
And while they pared, shaped, kneaded, rinsed and stirred,
they joyfully jostled, gossiped and laughed
feeling the bond of tradition that held them together.

Waiting, surrounded in the wings on the sideboard,
are heirlooms now graced with luscious pies, cakes and puddings,
spreading their own whiffs of delectable smells
to be savoured with Old King Cole in the best china cups.

Now the chairs are moving with animated children,
hungry for food and in anticipation of
re-acquaintance with cousins, kicking
each other under the table for fun.

Chairs filled with women, glowing with pride in the task well-done,
glad that part is over for at least this day;
and menfolk quietly content as providers of plenty.
Father, the Patriarch, now takes the limelight
while wielding the knife over turkey or ham,
while mother, the Matriarch, still fussing
over the slightest whim of her guests,
live their importance – their moment of glory
in thankfulness of all they received.

Ghosts and Deliverance

We were handcrafted with pride
from tallow and ashes. Dripping,
and counting on merciful angels, we guided
the children to beds in dark bedrooms –
we were the candles.

We did our best, while
women strained their eyes, stitching fine
heirlooms and hems, while pungent
vapours issued from our chimneys –
we were the oil lamps.

What more could we do?
Men tended the cattle and horses by
Flickering flames in dusky, dusty barns,
Risking their lives and their living –
we were lanterns.

My water was clear and pure.
Lonely women trudged-drudged
to partake in my bounty but without the vital,
life-assuring component of female companions
as in ancient times –
I was the bucket well.

I was forever needy, counting on
sturdy men and reluctant boys to fill me
so women could feed greedy stoves, so they
could cook nourishing foods for their families –
I was the wood box.

Jointly, we strung days and seasons
together like colourless beads on a string.
With power from oil, wood and water
we did our best –
we were the vassals.

Never we dreamed that those self-same powers
of tallow, oil, water and wood
so drudgingly dragged every day,
some day would provide ease through a wire, a
switch, and shiny devices
would save human labour, allow more leisure and
finer pursuits, more walks through the woods,
more cheer at the lake, more chats with neighbours –
and more food for the soul.

Wood Stove

I am Hestia – hearth, focus of home and household,
nourishing bodies and nourishing souls.
My black, polished, glimmering surface
allows foothold for singing kettles and simmering
stews in large pots,
filling the kitchen with savoury fragrances,
mingled with smells of baking bread and
burning wood,
assuring hungry stomachs of coming satisfaction.

The warmth from glowing coals and sparking wood
in my own belly draws folks like a
Pied Piper on cold winter nights,
spreading comfort through cold, bone-tired men folk,
allowing for casual chit-chat, blustery banter or
the peace that silence brings at day's end.

SENTINEL

I am one of many windows upstairs, facing northwest
in a favoured position, a boon in height and width,
unhampered vision, overlooking the road,
                                        the lake and
                                            far into the distant hills
grandly gorged by slow, persistent ice and water,
eons before my time.

Women often come to visit me, just to be,
to find solitude out of the hubbub downstairs,
giving thoughts to fancies and fears,
harking back to other times, other places, other lives,
dreams of desires, dares, doubts, dreads,
                    spinning languid longings, webs of wonder –
                                            musings on life's seasons.

Yet, at other times I share their quiet
reflections in the present, their pride and joy
in the laughter of children playing on the front lawn;
Billy pushing Cassia,
          Sophy swinging the swing,
                    Diana tripping Gary
                              Zöe catching a ball;

or

I share their joy in watching birds in bushes below
with their twittering, tittering antics;

or

their imaginings through watching daring, flitting bats
catching insects on the fly,
arousing images of broom-saddled witches in a moonlit sky;

or

their awe at flaming sunsets,
omen-filled firmaments,
riveting snowstorms,
driving rain,
stunning aurora borealis,
shafts of lightning;

or

cancelling fog.

Master Bedroom

First cry, last sigh;
these are my epiphanies:
Too often they became one.

My walls were often quiet witness
to Artemis hovering over a new life
ushered into the world with love and welcome
when all went well; with agony when not.

I saw my share of sickness, of trappings
and nostrums of combat, drawn-out recoveries,
miracle improvements, or ultimate slides into
the final resolution.

I witnessed masks being torn, shadows bared,
loading the air with dangerous offal
and, after catharsis completed, new
attempts at living love.

Yet most often my affinity engaged at the end
of day when downstairs all is done,
when tired bodies gladly enter, repose,
relax and reap the well deserved rest,
to rise again in the darkness
to another task-filled day.

BACK HALL

I am the center of beginnings and endings,
witness to most comings and goings,
hear sighs of relief after a hard day's work,
shouts of welcome to dear ones,
hear admonitions, advice and assurance to
those that depart from this home.

I receive all the mud, snow and debris
from pounding boots, discarded on the way
to the welcome kitchen,
catching all the cumbersome winter gear
thrown helter-skelter by boisterous youngsters
after their fun with toboggans and skates.

I hear happy chatter from lively kin,
anticipating festive dinners with
seldom seen clan,
chatty farewells after feasting is over,
and endings of stories that nourish
tradition and family ties.

Demeter nurtures expectations and seedlings
when sun-rays pour through
my south-facing window, long
before summer's nourishing heat in the garden
transforms seedlings into succulent produce:
and then

I play host to the bounty of garden and orchard
before skilled hands transform them into
preserves and security for next winter's tales.

Back Door

I, too, have two faces;
one facing the world, one facing
the hustle and bustle of home.

Like my counterpart out front
I'm hinged to keep out the unwanted
Or open wide to friendly folks.

I've been battered by rainstorms and sleet,
stood up against cold north-easterly winds,
gave entrance to scented spring breezes, bird song
and the robust clamour of children's sounds.

Second in rank, I feel first in command,
favoured to direct life's habitual traffic -
the comings and goings of Everyhuman,
threshold to common progression from youth to old age.

I am a yardstick of feelings,
handled all signs of emotions felt –
anger, fear, sorrow, joy.
I've been banged, barred, gripped, swung wide open.
My wounds are vivid and deep,
scars duly earned.

Most touching of all were those tiny hands -
my handle just within reach –
reaching for comfort or freedom
in defiance or anticipation,
eager or bashful,
trusting that, no matter what,
the solution lay waiting
on the other side.

EPILOGUE

I am old and decrepit, still,
no rattles and shakes;
there's life in me yet
I've got what it takes.

Many a generation did I shelter
many a season passed my nooks
many a storm has tested my mettle
many a change has changed my looks.

I am proud of my looks
and well I may be;
artist and poets were inspired
with paint, needle and words to honour me.

Time has transformed the needs of people,
though need for a home will always be.
I am proud and pleased to have been of service;
still, will the future have need of me?

The City and the Bay

City Bits

Fundy Bay, rocks and quay

Water rushing, sewers gushing

King's Square, fossils rare

Market stalls, shopping malls

Oil spills, steep hills

Giant tides, skidding rides

Irving bust, winter gusts

Burial ground, foghorn sound

Rockwood Park, lovers spark

Seagulls gliding, hunger hiding

Herring, shad, fish in shells

Smoke, smudge, smog, smells

Stark, staid, sturdy, stuck

Honour, loyalty, pride, pluck

Fundy City

Screaming seagulls, gracing changing skies,
Tracing arches from Bay to shore,
Echo a sombre city, facing Fundy's mighty roar.
Built by loyal subjects, sensing security
And greatness on the solid, rising rock.

Labour, confidence and faith raised this community,
Built lovingly its monuments to the now distant past.
King's Square and simple burial ground
Speak of loyalty and honour felt for king and kin.
Giant army barrack and grand fortress
Testify to a feisty, fighting spirit in case of need.
Eager market merchants and ferrying fishing fleet
Tell of busy barter and bustling crowds.
Smirking gargoyles and smiling cherubs
Show another, lighter side of these hardworking folks.

Ebb follows flood. Thunderous Fundy waters
Ram up the stately Saint John and the river reciprocates
with roaring regularity, bound by cosmic rhythms,
Giving shape and promise to life in this city,
As it did in the beginning. . .

Rockwood Park

I did not think
I would come back this time
with a poem worthy
of a name,
being preoccupied
with finding my way
in a maze of unmarked trails,
composing letters in my head to
the powers that be about
the dangers of losing tourists
in this gem of a park.

Until, finding my goal
- the other end -
and on my way back,
relaxed enough to see
this golden crown with
jewels like the yellow lady slippers,
bullhead water lilies,
cheerful cat's ears,

the ever-present dandelions
and a tiny snake, thinking
itself safe until I
toppled it's cover while
trying to sit on a stump.

And everywhere the
green of new summer and
marks of running life;
the sound of water
blown by the wind –
the miracles of Nature.

TWO-STEP 1999

At seven o'clock it is cold,

Polar cold on the Harbour Bridge, this pivotal evening when

Upright bundles of variegated height and colour amble towards its centre,

Eager for the blast of stars that will proclaim a major shift in numbers.

At midnight, by the water's edge – quiet.

Partridge Island lighthouse blinking its familiar code,

The bay strumming her slack-tide lullaby,

Ships as pencils lying at the horizon,

And after foghorns finish blasting their year-end greeting, stillness;

A stillness accenting the absence of bogus.

Here by the water, just another cold, calm night.

Sunday Morning Reflection

From where I sit,
Dirty scum, like old sheep's wool
Floats slowly into corners at the end
Of the harbour.

Five fishing boats rest, fluorescent pink and orange floats lie
Helter-skelter aboard, waiting for the men to steam away
Into cleaner and livelier waters, hoping for a decent catch
Of herring and cod.

Grey clouds hang heavy over black water and coastline,
Threatening rain.
Sparse Sunday traffic over the Harbour Bridge creates a steady hum,
A line of bikers a loud roar.

Walkers on the Cranberry Trail move according to need or purpose -
Fast, leisurely, run or ramble.
A mother trails her children through a maze
Of barrels on the other side.

Gulls fly free watching for a meal.
Three ducks float as if on a Sunday stroll.
A pleasure boat hurries in, heading for Pugsley Wharf.

Only yesterday, on this same spot,
The cruise ship "Carnival Victory" let loose
Some thousand revellers, happy to walk on solid ground,
Ready to see what they could see.

What they could see was our Loyalist City – settled by
Folks who loved the king.
At its centre, Kings Square, laid out like the Union Jack,
The Loyalist Burial Ground,
historic homes built by its prosperous merchants,
And a stately hotel, now serving as a home for older folks;

A large City Market under a vaulted roof like a 'turned over' boat
With various vendors selling produce and baked goods,
Souvenirs, snacks, coffee and fish, dulse, meat, poultry and eggs,
Jewellery, pottery, linens, spices and herbs, handicrafts and staples;

An old Carnegie Library, refurbished to show local art
To its best advantage, adding lectures, music and readings
To make the most of its possibilities –
A well-used jewel in this thriving town;

One short day is hardly enough to see Saint John's attractions.

Can't You Turn the Volume Down?

Arts Centre volunteering brings
Occasional treats for our auditory senses
When musicians hone talents
In preparation for an actual performance.

This time I am fortunate – a
Full voice rings through the hall, with
Clear, youthful exuberance, enhanced
By a keyboard doyen,
Attuned to each change in tempo and tone;
His ebullient resonance accentuates the graceful voice.

The telephone's discordant ring ruins the mood
And is quickly answered (that's what we are here for!).
The message, barely understood; repeats are requested, all ever so politely,
Until the woman on the other end, piqued, finally suggests
- Every so politely -
"Can't you turn the volume down?"

If I Could Talk To You…

and say what I want to say
I would tell you:

"Smile man, smile!
It is another day
fair or foul;
another day, yours to
make or break.
Those people are boarding,
with jobs to do, feelings,
commitments just like you, and me,
not just bodies filling the bus."

"Passengers – wake up!
Wake up! It's a person
behind the wheel,
not a robot controlling
fares and schedules."

"Each of us a part of human interaction
trying to belong,
forming community."
"Acknowledge one another –
be human."

Gallery Hop

From my home, walking through Market Square
up the escalator to Brunswick Square, I arrive
in the rain, to Handworks
with its jewellery, pottery and woodworks, all familiar.
Still, one special exhibitor – Amaterasa – slowed me down with her
legends-interpreting dishes, vases and bowls,
cheerfully coloured and fun-shaped,
telling stories with their comforting meanings for everyday life.
Through the back door to another art space
where a velvet and bisque angel, made by Dafina Mildenberger,
(which could be won by buying tickets)
reminded me that Christmas is on the horizon
(another one, already?).
Cards portraying the angel, photographed by Rob Roy
Are being sold by the sculptor
to benefit the local Special Loan Fund for artists. Then,
up some steps stood an inviting table, loaded with sweets and coffee,
and leading into Inprint, our independent bookstore,
where inside a preparation for a lecture, by William Forrester, a
sculptor
was in progress so
one could learn about the creation of his sculptures. -
A beautiful, satisfying evening.

MAY DAY

It's May Day, sunny and warming,
Dawn and dusk farther apart,
I feel more energetic, more alive.
The skate park is busier and
More people on the Harbour Passage.
Buds on the trees ready to open,
My dark blue pants are hot to the touch
But the breeze keeps me cool.
In the salt and pepper shaker homes on the boardwalk
People are making the most of the view,
Sitting on balconies with open windows.
Next door, occupants are sweltering
Behind construction plastic.
Flags wave lazily uptown.
The wharf is deserted.
The big white tent waiting
For eager tourists
Coming next month.
Before me the high wire-fence
With its barbed-wire top
Sends a strong message –
Stay out!

Behind me on the throughway
Traffic is light,
Which will change in an hour or so
When rush hour traffic
Takes over

I am going home
And make a cup of tea
to finish a pleasant afternoon.

Slack Tide Surprise

This morning, a bright detail worth sharing caught my fancy.

When I stepped out to greet the Bay, as usual,
I knew she would be there, as always
she has been, eons before I knew her.

Calm as could be she was,
caressing the seaweed-hung rocks with random laps,
boosting their primal scent.

Farther out, black rocks spot her surface,
placidly watching her changing tides.

At the horizon, like slugs attached to her dark grey skin,
lie the supertankers; only slightly darker than the new grey sky.

Seagulls come and go,
perching and soaring, screaming their ancient codes.

All I noticed were pencil shades of grey,
until, looking down,
I startled to a wider palette, seeing
the bright yellow coltsfoot at my feet.

BEACHCRAFT

The beach is empty
but for the signatures of
earth's birthing pains;
working with wind and water
through time,
oblivious to the consequences
and observing eyes.

Ancient folds of rock formations
like pastry dough
play havoc with our sense
of possibilities.

Split rocks with imprints
of age-old leaf and beetle
show just how long
this sculptress has amused herself
with stone and living creatures,
challenging our rock-hard
certainties.

Rock faces carved
through untold storms
are hung
with frosty lace-curtains;
an unwashed white with
hushed pink blush,
as if embarrassed to be
flung out so suddenly
to public exposure.

Farther down the beach she has created
swords of Damocles
which crash with sudden speed
on the boulders below,
freed by the warming sun.

Where ocean waters meet the shore
waves of ages have created other marvels;
mixed with elemental grey
are countless surprises,

of curious shapes and shades,
transformed by human imagination into
a slice of liver, a chunk of cheese,
a speckled egg of an exotic bird.

Pure white and mottled greens, brindled browns,
deep purple, fragile pink, shiny black and
freckled multi-colour forms compete for
our attention.

Where rocks reach out into the surf
and put an end to our stroll,
rock goodies on a sand-stone tray
of sun-warmed rust
seem hastily thrown together
by a truant hostess…
Did she expect observers after all?

SANDY FERNS

Sandy ferns, messed about

By footprints of gulls and varied

Footwear, mingle

Between diverse beach stones.

Greying sky surrounds the sinking

Sun; rough, curling waves, encouraged

By the sea wind, separate the granite

Bay from the silvery beach

Prior to the darkness of night.

STORMY THOUGHTS

Strings of cormorants animate the sky until
blending into the wooded cliffs
or dropping out of sight in the darkened bay.

Rumbling stones add their own voice, while
the lid of storming skies highlights the crashing, hissing surf,
pushing the pungent, putrid sea smells up shore.

Dapper fighters for survival on these rugged cliffs,
maddening winds ruffle roses
lupins, daisies and grasses –

Winter Sky

Wispy pulp mill clouds scud by,
not even surviving the width of my window,
a lifespan of minutes in this cold, cold weather,
dropping the dross of their being
into the air we breath.

WINTER GARGOYLES I

Anchored solidly
on tide-battered rocks,
stoically facing the coastal slope,
a momentary creation of icy gargoyles
with backs defiantly turned
to their creator,
as if their existence has been,
and will forever be,
receiving her additions
of freezing spray;
good-naturedly,
subtly, changing their countenances.

Winter Gargoyles II

Icy creatures, anchored on the tide-battered rocks,
Stoically facing the coastal slope;
Momentary creations, whimsical gargoyles,
Backs defiantly turned to their creator - the bay -
As if their existence has been and will be forever
Good-naturedly receiving fresh freezing spray.
Subtly changing countenances,
Scraggly beards, slit eyes,
Mis-formed mouths, droopy tusks;
Different expressions, adding further
Variant fancies in my mind.

Slack Tide

Scum skitters up rough rocks
Seals slip-slide from black hummocks
The slate Bay watches

Spring Fever

The Bay is skittish this morning
- like a racehorse too long waiting –
slapping and flapping short rollers on the shore
as if she too is eager to get involved with
the affairs of this new spring.

Afterthought

The roar

came with me

when I left the Bay

Flora, Fauna, Weather

Soul Grabbers

It was the trees that grabbed my soul.
Various features of this homestead caught my attention
while home-hunting that cold winter day.
The simple fireplace (a warming focus),
the views from the windows also enticing,
as was the space
for the children to grow and explore.

But it was the trees that grabbed my soul,
placed in a graceful curve, sentinels
filled with stories
of many lives, of times long past.
Rooted solidly, assuring an anchor
in stormy gales.
Tall trunks, not to be girded by mere humans,
raised heaven-ward their mighty arms
supporting in three of our seasons
leafy umbrellas reaching over the roof of the home
we sought,
sheltering countless creatures year after year,

encouraging the multitude
into ensuring their next generation while
they cast shadows over rambunctious roses, and
promising wild, roaring reverberations
during seasonal furies, enticing
my mind into brooding tales
of ghosts and ghouls.

It was the trees that grabbed my soul.

Fall In The Air

"The sound stops short, the sense flows on."
Chinese saying

I

Honking convivially, announcing their passage
long before they come in sight.
V-ing geese, playing tag,
pointing south, like snowbirds
who mimic their trek, outsmarted by goose
instinct.

II

Announcing their passing,
V-ing geese honk amiably
like chatty women in kitchens preparing
communal meals, while men discuss baseball scores,
beer in hand, on the back porch,
anticipating concoctions the women prepare.

Geese, unburdened by this routine,
wind down at dusk, worn and hungry
to devour grass-seeds, weeds,
and rest in sheltering hayfields.

REMEMBER EARLY OCTOBER

Remember early October,
Sunday silence,
a gift of beauty, of wellness,
of maple's colour, bustling squirrels,
wasps romping on sun-drenched pavement,
chipmunks on the lawn gathering nuts,
stark-blue skies, V-ing geese,
falling fruit, pungent with fermenting juices -
a day to be savoured, saved against
raw November.

A Change In The Air

Damaged daisies dangle on still sturdy stems
in soggy soil.
Clusters of purple fall asters, half closed by cold.
Brave rosebuds – doomed to stillbirth.

Slowly autumn advances.
Geese flew South some time ago.
Apple orchards empty of harvest,
only lately abandoned.
Leaves changed colour, now steadily dropping.
Darkness comes early.
Meals on the table, under lit lamps.
It seems a dreary season, still, fascinating and
full of its own beauty,
full of promise of what's to come -
brilliant snow on branches and roadways,
mix of blessing and curse,
until the axis tilts at Winter Solstice,
starting a new cycle of change into spring.

Misnomer

Butterfly

Breezy gauze

Winged palette

Flashy forager –

More aptly named

Flutterby

By my

Son

Lamentation

In our neighbourhood, our streets are graced with maple trees
planted after the houses were built – homes for soldiers coming
back after duty in a cruel war.

The trees grew with the families,
wheeling through the cycle of seasons, growing
from soft, whispery greens on springy twigs to
dense, full crowns like sovereign territories,
with homes for countless creatures, full of promise and ambition.
The trees rooted solid, as if meaning to stay while families made homes,
grew up and moved on to other quests.

Each autumn these maple trees, like
rakish fools in a pageant, displayed their
famous, flaming colours.

This year, this flaming show - like a no-show -
made no appearance; instead, blight doused the flames,
blight swallowed the colours, devouring beauty,
discarding leaves as black as tarred bullets, clusters plop down
loaded, heavy with the premonition of doom.

Last Survivor

|
|
|
|
|

There it hung, one surviving oak leaf,
lone hanger-on from last year's bounty,
a bronze pirouette
twirling like a whirligig,
fighting a force fierce enough
to topple trees.
Hour after hour
a ferocious fighter, held by one
invincible strand, determined
not to yield, Dylan-like
until it must
to let life
go on.

UNRULY

Unconventional,

looking unlike others of your kin,

you stand straight, opening just so much,

fading, falling apart, dying.

No, not at all like a tulip,

you opened extravagantly,

standing spread-eagled,

rising from a diaphanous glass, proudly

showing your blazing sun-yellow private parts,

your petals resembling slender,

dried-blood coloured hexapods,

or grotesque arachnids.

You share space with pale pinkish cousins,

dried, shrivelled dumplings; not even so much as pretending

to be glad to feel spring.

Upon Awakening

The winter neighbourhood awakens
and empties out while
I watch, drinking my first mug of tea.

Streetlights dim one by one,
cars back out of driveways – people
heading to their daily affairs elsewhere.
Sleepy teens drag bags of papers door to door.
Children walk to school, quietly,
preparing their futures but not quite
ready for an active day.

Overhead, hungry gulls fly north
from the Bay to feeding grounds,
leaving me, the cats and dogs,
the scurrying squirrels and cawing crows
and
the weather.

Winter Haiku

Mushy snow hiding
treacherous icy patches
deceived walkers

Slowly winter creeps
from its solstice towards
spring's equinox

PLAINT

I long for a warm, wild storm from the south;
Winds that whip the Bay into action, chase her complacency, her
Peaceful lapping the shore as if that's all.

I hate those storms that keep coming
From the west in relentless regularity.

I resent the need for winter gear and second-hand heat,
Walking canes and ice-picks and fear of falling.

I hate waking in the morning again and again
To yet another fresh blanket of white.

I know I am forgetting winter's beauty, its peace,
Its awe-inspiring presence, its hoar frost,
Its winter enthralments of snow-walks and glittering moonscapes and,
Yes, I also know….

The robins are back, braving the cold, forever hopeful.
I see some new greens grow in tiny, sunny spaces –
Yet still sadly surrounded by droopy, dirty old snow-banks.

I know too the days are longer, the bitter cold
No more, that spring is here.

Still, is it too much to wish for a wild storm in the Bay
To chase away this long and brutal winter?

WINDS, WATER, WEATHER

We have storms to relish, fear, remember,
warranting attention, response;
memorable by their strength and determination,
seemingly set on destruction and mayhem,
throwing and blowing leaves and debris,
flipping and whipping umbrellas, ripping them free
from gripping hands for a dance in the sky.

Storms rippling puddles, challenging windbreaks,
trees and ships, battling rushing rivers and white-capped
lakes, bays and oceans, storms bent on having their way.

Dead Crow

There, in the gutter, she lies
neatly on her back,
wings and feet folded,
prim and ready as if
waiting for an open casket,
while overhead her mourners
call their distress:
There, but for the Grace of Life,
am I.

Ode To Tobi

Little rascal
with your grinning smile
tireless, trusting,
faithful, smart,
keen, lively,
loving and lovable,
inquisitive rock hound
(what was the charm of these rocks,
so quietly carried for hours?).
A three-legged champion,
larger in courage than your attackers
who were wimps.

You gave so much joy
to all who knew you –
a tribute to a loving home.
Your death left a scorching hole in our hearts
that only time can heal.

So good to have known you Tobi;
you will never be forgotten.

Cat's Caper

Weaving through the balustrade of Lucille's farmhouse
like we wove little mats in kindergarten,
like mending socks now that we are staid,
like a maniac weaving at rush hour,
Spice, the cat, closes in on Floppy, the dog,
sitting with ears alert for the familiar sound of Lucille's car,
unaware of her rival's upcoming prank.

Speculative Spring

Yellow spots of coltsfoot brighten the
greening grass along the path.
Sticky buds test the air, stirred by the cool, brisk wind,
and feel a promise of warmer spring day's coming.
The Bay, pushing white caps up the shore, invites
a restful contemplation on the bench, supplied by a caring bay watcher.
Alas! His generous gift hangs broken, a wanton wreckage,
work of a wild, destructive vandalism.
Abashed, I walked on, wondering who would find
pleasure in such reverse industry.
A black cat, out for a stroll, crosses my path, maybe,
like me, to see what changes
spring has shaken from her sleeve.

The Travail of Life

GRONINGEN 1937

Whitewashed sneakers on the kitchen windowsill,
ready for next day Sunday school.

Walking to school with my best friend Elsje, playpen-bonded playmate,
more dear than a sister.

Men on their knees with heavy canvas kneepads, replacing
broken red bricks on the sidewalk or straightening
cobblestones in the roads carrying the heavier traffic.

Men in heavy canvas halters trudging along on sloping paths along the canals,
pulling their barges, loaded with peat or sugar beets.

Men on bridges with wooden poles, an 'oude klomp' at the end,
swinging it down to collect the toll for lifting the bridge so the barges can pass.

Men manoeuvring the chutes to load or unload barges with wheat or rye.

Men walking on the unstable mass in the holds of the barges,
keeping the chutes immersed.

The beautiful colours of oil spills in the busy canals.

Lamplighters with long steel rods, lighting the gas lamps at dusk,
just like the teacher in the classroom in winter.
Seeing a newspaper float by on the breeze,
with four-inch headline announcing the death of Paus Pias with a Roman numeral.

Being in love with the sound of Paus Pias, Paus Peeas…

Skating

First ice, safe enough to hold skaters,
means an extra holiday afternoon from school!
Students run home to make the most of it,
maybe their only chance in our mild climate.

When I arrive, I see droves of eager
schoolmates testing out their rusty skills,
some already far away, striding toward distant goals.
Close by, mothers attend young ones, binding skates,
holding hands or guiding
supporting chairs.
I come late, making my way to the nearest canal,
trudging reluctantly, skates dangling
from shoulders, resentment glowing from my face.
Alone, as friends joined the crowd long ago,
deserting me in my misery which is mine alone –

I HATE SKATING!

HERFTE, THE NETHERLANDS, MAY 10, 1940

"*Anna, they came,*
I saw them marching,
their tanks crawling along like
some beastly barbarian."
Anger sputtering his speech,
my father walked in, slamming the door.

Close to middle age, balding, tall,
his muscular frame dressed casual,
he flaunted his forceful presence.

"*Where? I hear nothing, Heiko,*" my mother replied,
suddenly yanking my hair she was braiding.
Still in her housecoat, small, neat but harried,
she urged us kids, all four of us, to hurry.

"*I heard they bombed Rotterdam,*
dropping troops by parachute –
thousands of them.
All our men are over there;
no one and nothing to defend us here," father added.

"*I thought we were neutral,*" mother offered.

"*Not anymore, Hitler decided for us.*"

He sat down restlessly,

glancing at his four kids bustling about

in preparation for school.

"*Come, I'll show you,*

at the railroad crossing

we can see them, way over

on the Veeralee, marching to town;"

muttering "*those misbegotten Moffen,*"

under his breath.

"*Your better not go to school today,*" my mother said,

securing my braid with a ribbon.

First Move Of Many

My mother, coping with a brood of four,
picking and packing in a crowded flat,
shoved us roughly out the door after
a hasty half-breakfast,
not hearing our question: "Can we get a ride?"

We crowded on the stoop, watching
our stuff being carried out into
broad daylight for all to see; every
passer-by and nosy window watcher judging,
pooh-poohing or admiring.

Two men - one grey and harried, the other
tall and shabby – commanded by my splendid father,
pushed and shoved the whole caboodle
into a cart, while its horse –
a brown and sagging, patient creature,
safely tucked between the shafts –
flicked its tail at bothersome flies.

The big question we had asked
hung around us like a sheet of fog,
slowly turning into dampening drizzle of pleasure denied.
No treat for us – "Sorry kids, no room left."

And so we walked …

into a new horizon…

WALKING HISTORY LESSON ON THE WAY TO SCHOOL

I used to walk

From country home ———————————— to city school

and always late, I rushed through history - - -

Leaving my home, I make a
left turn at our garden gate and see
across the sandy path
the old forest surrounding
the baron's treasured estate –
barbed wire denoting
his privileged rights.

I hurry past my greengrocer neighbour
loading his wagon
with fresh handpicked produce, while
his horse takes a last nibble of hay
before their round begins.

Next I pass a Jewish burial ground, deserted –
its potential occupants
now thrown into pits
due to the sick sense of justice
of one warped soul.

At the end of the path another
sharp left onto the macadam –
built, as folklore tells us,
by Roman Legions of olden days – I rush
under ancient oaks, their soaring crowns
hiding the sky, their mighty trunks
hinting at age-old travellers,
whispered secrets of timeless lovers,
vagabonds, and
German invaders
as recently as last night's moon.

Then, shortly, after a sharp turn to the right
I see the sky once more, and pass
through a wooden gate into lush pastures freshly
flecked and scented with flops of cow manure.

Hurrying over a cinder footpath,
I jump three ditches or
am helped across by single boards
depending on the season.
Arriving at last at the last gate,
I enter a greengrocer's dream
and pass neat plots of varied hues and textures,
loam-scented and worked with care and
pride for peak and prime return.

Without a break, I am within the city limits -
wide streets and modern homes denote
the newness of the scene –
until I cross by drawbridge
into a maze of narrow streets from days of long ago.

Narrow row-houses complement the small and
varied stores, all sparsely stocked -
a scarcity that will increase with every trainload of goods
heading east into the land of
what we called, the Moffen.
Gothic churches watch over the markets,
their shape reflecting its flock's faith in the Cross.
Tall steeples and stained glass windows
add a touch of elegance to the scene.
The once joyous carillons
still mark the passing of time, but
the familiar wind-whipped hymns
and patriotic melodies are,
temporarily (we are certain),
replaced by German sentiments.

The markets used to be active places on market days,
but that too has changed. There used to be
lively merchants praising their wares, some
in traditional costume speaking
colloquial speech to
bustling shoppers searching carefully
for necessities, haggling good-naturedly,
and going home well satisfied.

Hurrying on, I meet and pass
fellow walkers and lucky cyclists and,
then, singing, marching fodder,
so proud of their shiny black boots
of which the droning resonance
implies to them their power.
And then I am shocked to see
a shackled, valiant compatriot
who should, like me,
be on his way to school,
but who, instead, most likely
will never see again that
seat of learning – and I know
that power lies in courage, not boots.
I thank him silently.

In my hurry, I almost collide
with a woman on a ratty old bike
its brakes not working,
bare to the rims.
She is smart; who in their right mind
would bring out a newly polished bike,
outfitted to a tee,
only to have it
grabbed from under you
by a hoggish, haughty Quisling?

An antiquated city gate by
a star-shaped moat leads me over
another drawbridge out of
this old Hansa town and almost
to my destination – but not before
yet another half-run to
yet another bridge, and this one closed

serving as a lame excuse
for being late – once more.

"Look At This; Do You Remember?"

Do I remember? How could I forget this
home, this shelter against tyranny?
Four years of fear, safety, hunger, danger, wants and needs in this
small abode of brick walls, stone floors, without plumbing,
facing an ancient oak forest, part of a baronial estate.
A home filled with parents and siblings, with courage and ethical choices.

This home – pictured here so prim, so light, *so right*.
I knew it in what seems another lifetime when
it sheltered Jews against the Final Solution, and
young minds against arrogance about "their" Reich, their
claim on our sovereignty. It sheltered
clandestine BBC news with supportive Royal voices.
It sheltered my innocence and dreams about freedom,
sheltered my first leap into romantic love – until …

A traitorous voice set us to running
an ominous journey, finding shelter with strangers and
chancy safety until our flag flew free again.

This pivotal home between girl and woman,
between innocence and knowing
between prison and freedom – how could I forget?

Know

Know Thou Shalt Not Kill

Life is sacred, God's Image

Mass graves dot the world

My Mother Anna

She died long before she died - my mother.
Her body hanging in there after her spirit left.
No, not Alzheimer, nor senility,
nor any of those dread diseases
that leave us bereft of all our senses.
Instead, her creativity, her energy, her full range of senses,
her own mind, her sense of self - lost.

She used to be so brave, so full of energy and story,
so full of answers to our growing needs,
so full of love, of hope.
I did not know her then,
too young to know of things like that.

A woman's spirit can only take so much
of stymied needs and lack of love,
giving all without a sign of thanks,
of harsh and sarcastic words,
her goodwill taken for granted.

She was no saint but very much a woman
who paid for being a woman - her spirit
turned sour in an acidic atmosphere.

Debt

I am here still…
Fulfilled my female fecundity
Smelled my newborn's primal scent
Still do…
Now, from ensuing generations.
Filled three score and ten …and more, still
Tasting freedom
Feeling love and betrayal
Eating from the apple
Following dreams
Earning grief and mourning, still
walking into my kismet: However,
in my shadow there are graves of others who
gave their lives for strong-felt canon, forfeiting
their futures, freedoms
feelings of betrayal
relinquishing their progeny
smelling their newborns' primal scent…
so I could live?

My Mountains

Once upon a time
I moved mountains ....
I moved mountains of laundry and
mountains of dough for
mountains of bread and
I moved mountains of dishes from
mountains of meals and
I moved mountains of dirt from
mountains of boot trails
I moved mountains of challenging changes and
mountains of dull dreary deadness
I moved mountains of hurts and
moved mountains of tears
I moved mountains of failures and
mountains of triumphs
creating peaks of jubilation and
valleys of regret.

And while I was moving those mountains
the sun bathed my landscape in light,
the moon gave new light in the darkness,
fogs muffled the sounds and the fury within me,

rains washed the mountains afresh,
winds blew air through the crannies,
storms howled their courage through charged air
while mudslides and cave-ins and torrents
shaped my mountains forever anew.

And now when I look at that landscape
shrouded in a fog of hazy memory,
enlightened by hindsight and truth,
I know I moved mountains
that had to be moved.

LAUNDRY FANCIES

Long line of laundry, leaping,
reaching, releasing future rain
stories, blowing in the wind.
Love-tucked sheets,
pillow cases with wisps of forgotten dreams,
(and hiding the unmentionables?)
dish towels reminiscing about sparkling dishes,
fine-cut wineglasses, saucy soup bowls, elegant entrée platters,
dainty dessert dishes but, mostly
cobbled everyday stuff.

Fabulous blouses, telling T-shirts, stylish skirts,
slender and not-so slacks.
And did I mention the unmentionables?

The items that have seen better days;
hard-worked work shirts,
patched jeans, mended socks and
those sundry, uncoded objects, all
with wagging tattle - tales of watching struggles,
joys, adventures …

If only they could speak.

Old Sheets

Holes from tickled toes
Rubbing shoulders, hips, kisses –
Sheets worn with love.

FAMILY PLATE

Was I, after all,
only the glue that held the
plate together after the crash?
The plate I knew worthy, worth saving
for further use, worth all I had and was
worthy of becoming a family heirloom. But glued,
it shows its faulty form, each piece broken into
its own faulty form, each piece broken into
its own peculiar shape, splinters and chips
missing, joy, innocence, trust, respect, unity;
all that gave the plate its value. The glue,
with bubbles of fear, missing at spots, and
t o o t h i n l y s t r e t c h e d i n
others, could not undo the damage, gloss
over the pain. And when the glue gave
out, the plate's real substance was
laid bare – bro ken pie ces of a
beau ti ful pl ate now
broken beyond repair.

Metamorphosis

Take me, for instance,
anchored in an old cocoon;
brains out, eyes unseeing,
nose numb, mouth shut,
shoulders stuck, heart and guts caught
in the rim.
Legs noosed;
a mature, full-grown body
snared by fear far too long until…
something gave – a twinge, a nudge,
a stirring, a tiniest tremor in my toe.
So it moved – just a fleeting start,
mobilizing power, spreading energy through
muscle and blood
until the feet – thrusting, pushing, pressing -
propelled me to freedom,
finally thinking, finally seeing,
smelling, giving voice,
moving, feeling, acting,
able to walk…
now what do I do?

Jealousy

My leg trap –

a demon jerking me back

a fury yanking my hair

a monster gulping my juiciest tidbits

I keep throwing him

I tease him like a flirt

pulled by the rogue's strings

ON TIPTOES

Tiptoeing through the
Minefield of my buried emotions
I try to detonate them
Softly …
Without pain
Without upheaval
Exposing my unknown past
Ending my fear without
Turmoil …
Without disturbing my
Status quo

It won't work.

MIJNVELD *

Zachtjes, op mijn tenen,

schuifel ik door het nijnveld

van mijn begraven emoties –

probeer ze te detoneren

zonder pijn

zonder omwenteling –

prober mijn ongekende jeugd

te exposere -

mijn vrees te eindigen

zonder verwarring

zonder mijn status quo

te raken

het gaat niet.

* *On Tiptoes* in Dutch

Dawn Insight

Hydro wires crisscrossing the beauty
of dawns and dusks
impeding their unbounded expanse
I know is there.

And I, like a drunkard,
lost in a haze
of hurts that eat me alive,
like an alcoholic who craves
blame and self-pity to
nourish the wounds
inflicted by life gone sour –
impeding my new beginnings;

the opening future.

LIBERATION

One gull, single keeper of the sky,

Testing her mettle

Against the storm,

Taking my jealousies,

Worn out and dangerous,

Tearing them into

Infinite fragments,

Thus rendering them clawless –

Setting me free.

Full Circle

Once upon a time
I sat amidst confusion
Trying to still my mind
With red crosses upon white linen,
Designing order in the thick of chaos.

My aunt was pleased,
For her, my labour lent cachet
To simple dishes.

Life's autumn intervened
And sent the gift back to me.
Now, in the turning of my life
They tell me
Once before
Once upon a time
I managed order out chaos.

NEW HOME

My new home…

a place to live

as best I can.

I care for it and

enjoy the freedom it provides

a place to come and go

but nothing more.

Love it? Attachment?

Why should I?

It would become a trap again

and doom me to another

searing scar that holds me

back from growing.

Regret

I wanted good for each and every child;
tried making happy childhoods, inspiring tempers mild enough
to stop and listen for the songs of birds
yet strong enough to tackle tough decisions.

I failed – as any human must -
loaded with old mores, ignorance, misplaced trust.
I counted too soon on yet to be acquired skills
unknowingly setting the stage for disaster.
I wanted so much that sorrow should pass by
my children – at least until some sense of worth
and fairness had developed to avoid disasters,
to know when trust and fairness were not in the picture.

My Existence

My existence now is as useless as

a broken flowerpot,

ready to crumble back into the earth

where it came from.

Once a vessel of plenty, filled with beauty, nurturing soil,

alive with healthy nitrogen, aerating, crawling annelids,

active sprouting, growing, maturing,

holding beautiful

prolific produce,

each to its own kind;

and, now, each one independent,

living according to their unique possibilities.

And so, now my pot is lingering,

useless, in a fancy holding shed.

IT SEEMS

It seems, suddenly
kin and friends slipped away without notice,
as if no connection ever existed;
letters not answered, not returned;
phones out of service – leaving a void of not knowing.

Our pasts were joined, playpen shared, lives lived close in
shared secrets, giggly talks, familiarity and participation.
We shared a neighbourhood, schools, teachers;
parents were "owned" mutually.
After moving away, letters kept us joined.
We knew about each other's boyfriends, dates, intimacies.
And later, we knew about each other's offspring, and
the next generations. We exchanged pictures and stories as proud
mothers and omas, so…
Did she leave no address book, no phone list? After she died?

It feels as if I made her up, a fantasy figure whom,
as I grew older, abandoned me.

Reuse, Recycle, Reclaim

Its lacuna held liquid I quaffed.

Red and yellow daisies cheering the outer surface;
A smaller version inside
Winks back at me whenever I take a sip.
A small daisy chain graces its handle.
Shaped like a stubby, fat candle, it is
A comfort to hold; its warmth permeates
My hands on cold winter days, following
Long walks or shovelling the driveway.

My favourite mug, until
I chipped it in my hurry and lubberly ways.

Now it stands, rendering repose
To pencil, pen and highlighter,
Reminding me of Jolena, granddaughter, gift bearer
On that particular Christmas.

Navel Gazing

It just sits there; center stage. Useless now, but…

A mark of distinction, a medal for our successful struggle
Between an end and a beginning;
The end of the greatest security we'll every know,
A breaking of a journey to an independent self;
A fight, abandoning the safety of our nave.

A given with every mammal birth, still,
Each unique as snowflakes drifting down.

A sign of loss, a knot in our skin, tying up lose ends,
A final touch, a birthmark, a dot as in a child's
'connect-the-dots' picture – tracing
the umbilical cord, linking first ancestor with last descendant.

Belly button – an apt metaphor – but how limiting, prosaic,
Its profound crux lost in a word.
Just sitting there, yet proving the most vital link
Between a mother and her child;
Her arms, her love, her care will never be quite equal
To the former innate closeness, the being two in one.

It just sits there; center stage, anatomy in a nutshell;
Final touch to complete a being – a medal.

PARENT GRIEF

So swift from joy to woe, your first and last,
Your only child. One time your life was thrilled
With longing expectations; they richly filled
Your days. First joyful clue, first youth flew past,
Graced life – so rich, so frightfully fast.
At Equinox, his last, the cancer killed.
Your future destroyed. Your loss so vast,
Worse than any other grievous blow
Tormenting humankind. Your faith
In fairness, God – all lost their dazzling glow.
Instead, a sadness penetrates your strife
To understand, accept unholy woe;
No joy, but just this ever-wrenching knife.

Shifting Rank

My first great-grandchild
extends the family line, linking forward
just as my "opoe"
whom I remember but vaguely –
reaches back as far as my memory goes.
Beyond her, my line is lost in the common past.

For now, I hold the middle ground of knowing
three back, three forward,
while once I was its blank beginning.

I am now its oldest link.
Slowly, inevitably, positions shift
farther back until
I, too, get lost in the common past.

Portraits

THEODORUS VAN GOGH

I sired two Vincent Willem's;
one lives – why him?

Out of progeny of six, five fitted fairly,
but Vincent's indecent fiendish being was bane on me.

He soured my fatherhood,
grinding amity like grist.

He shamed my ministry
with wild abandoned zeal.

He made wild, crude pictures, painted in a frenzy,
blinding colours – never sold one.

My shoes, clean and decent, sketched as
two clumps, as if belonging to a crofter.

He begs coin from brother Theo;
softer than a woman – his only ally.

Chasing wenches, he shames
God-fearing kin and other folks.

A barking dog, chasing windmills,
wet paws puddling all encounters.

An alien in a fine flock –
I shall never comprehend.

On A Self-Portrait Of Hilaire Germain Edgar Degas 1834-1917

Tipping your hat midway – on or off?
Gloves at the ready –
Coming or going? Where?
Your eyes too pensive
For a rendezvous with a lover
- Just past or yet to come –
Your stance too relaxed.

It wouldn't be the beach now,
Would it?
Your joys are differently focused;
Urban scenes,
'Key-hole' visions of
women cleaning themselves 'like animals',
combing hair, stretching limbs in dance
to the limits of endurance.

The opera maybe?
An Impressionist exhibition?

Horses and racetrack – there too
The magic of legs.
Just observing yourself, judging?
Debonair, witty, misanthrope, blindness
Not yet envisioned.

This Is My Charlotte

Small in stature but mighty in spirit –
adventurous artistic
and bold
caring creative crone
daring and dancing
energetic
and fun
generous gardener and 'grandmother'
humble humorous
ingenious involved
jokester
kind and knowing
loving
mighty
no nonsense
observant
practical poet
quiet
rhythmic
spiritual strong tough
undaunted
vigourous
witchy witty warrior
exceptional
yogi
zany at times but always admirable

William Prouty

Ambrosial feasts

Eclectic circles

Master, mentor -

William

Reputation: A Fantasy

pot smoking
sex-crazy at the beach
men-stalking
drug addicts
black humour movies –
very bad things
such is my reputation now

I used to be so nice
I used to be so good
I used to be so obliging
I used to be so right
and oooh so straight
such was my reputation then

correct – corrupt
vice – virtue

shedding fetters
flying wild
tasting
choosing
experimenting
breaking my mould
leads to becoming me
the best reputation yet

Tongue In Cheek

For such a modest looking flap of muscle,
the tongue is quite a busy piece of art.
Starving without its first help in sucking,
we would have stopped right then and there.
We cannot eat, or taste, or chew without it.
And what about our speech?

Tiny taste buds festooning its rim hold
warnings, invitations, pleasures and smarts.
Its unimpressive colour, nonetheless, holds clues
about our state of health.
It fits snugly in its allotted berth, yet
can reach far out, double up, pick teeth,
poke fun, insult, lick, rrrrroll and
has an integral part in making love.

We may bite our tongue,
hold our tongue,
have a sharp tongue,
speak tongue-in-cheek or
be tongue-tied.
We may try tongue twisters,
receive or give tongue-lashings,
or cause other peoples tongues to wag.
For such a modest looking flap of muscle,
the tongue is quite a busy piece of art.

A Box Full Of Questions

A souvenir from foreign shores
Made for the tourist trade.
What energy of nimble hands
Went into making this tiny box?
What thoughts and feelings filled this treasure?
Did she ponder why these distant beings
Had a need for objects like this bagatelle?
Did she wonder what trinkets, treasures, treats
Would fill its hollowed space?
Did she choose its colours, its design?
Did she enjoy the labour or
Would she rather walk or cook or read or play
Or simply sit and wonder?
What filled her craft – concerns, joys, dreams,
Resentment, apathy, nothingness?
Were the rewards in keeping with her needs and worth?
How old was she, or maybe he?

Troubling questions for questing minds;
Most answers known or surmised through print, images, voices
And still we buy.

Bread I

Our breaking bread, the blessed, sacred act:
A pledge to satisfy our need for grace,
Community rapport, a living pact
Between a higher power and the human race.
In fertile fields men sow and reap the grain.
In homely kitchens women knead the dough.
Concerted toil and common goals sustain
An atmosphere in which affinity will grow.
Community births the offspring able
To satisfy an honest hunger earned
Through forthright work, and blessings at the table.
A simple meal suffices, all fancies spurned.
Their gratitude, respect, and skills decreed
Their faith in humble bread, and God agreed.

Bread II

"Give us this day our daily bread" has now
become an order rather than a plea.
Where nature once was Queen and led the plough,
We now have progress King, and ethics flee.
The ears of grain upreaching, whole, God's hands.
Now selfsame grain, all grown in endless fields.
Still reaching up, still whole, but serving wants,
Not needs, but greed in charge and forcing yields.
Senseless monsters work while nature groans.
Home labour lost; the smells, the taste, all dead.
Now factory ovens spewing forth neat clones,
Creating lifeless carbohydrate – Wonder Bread -
While bread as symbol lost its worth
And work its pride, we smothered Mother Earth.

A Skein Of Wool

A skein of wool;
an airy pretzel,
its colour stolen from the sky
with a bury-your-face-in softness
and warmth, as if
still in unison with its creator,
the sheep,
still part of the bartering system -
protection for yield.

A skein of wool;
each generation knowing three
doing the same.
All part of the chain, creating goods and memories
of caring;
sharing frustration with contrary needles and jumbled yarn
in small clumsy fingers
and victory with the first recognizable scarf.
Mothers with youngsters needing
a steady supply of woolly winter wear,
warm and cosy.

Grandmother looking back,

remembering her own frustrations, victories, endless needs,

now in peace that all was done

that could be done.

A skein of wool;

a thread connecting generations

far back into antiquity

and reaching forward

tentatively -

not sure about its destination.

The Woodworker's Shop

This ample aerie is art by innuendo.
Windows frame old Dutch paintings, say – a van Ruisdael, or a Cuyp.
A warm sheen bounces from its pine walls
like everlasting light.

A straight mini-forest stands waiting in a corner:
planks of tanned oak, rich birch, white pine,
scented cedar, while at their feet
stands a basket filled with odd chunks of scarcer,
exotic wood – ebony, rich walnut, dark mahogany, bird's eye maple,
imported from imagined shores.

Wide-eyed whatnots watch a humming lathe on which
the mix of miniature vases they hold, found form.
Chisels hang like sorted soldiers on a wall,
marking time until their services are needed.

Coping saws form a Cubistic drawing on another wall and
piles of aromatic shavings conjure
intricate Victorian coiffures.

Dusty the cat sleeps wisely in fragrant sawdust dunes,
under the work table.

The Exercise of Joy

BOOTS

Next to life itself,
surely,
boots must be the
best friend in all creation,
at least on days like this –
raw wind and pouring rain.

Without these sleek, slim escorts
my woodsy walk would be nothing but
a stream of frets
about cold, wet feet and
dire consequences.

Yet, with these boots,
thoughts are free
to sway with the wind,
perch on the rain streaks
that drum-beat my back or
tickle my face into grins.
They blind me to all but my
primary goal of
feeling alive.

I Don’t Know Where She Came From

Suddenly there she was,
a little yellow lentil.
At close up,
a lemon-yellow happy face
with spider legs
hanging from the china cabinet,
dangling on her gossamer strand,
taking her chances
her own way.

I had been packing
for a move,
taking things from a dark closet,
disturbing long forgotten relics.
Did she cling to one of these?

I don’t know where she came from
but she made my day.

PICKING THE LAST BLUEBERRIES

Six groping hands,
six searching eyes,
two squatting bodies, relaxed;
one bending awkwardly, tense.
Still, all of one mind – to find
those last sweet berries of the season.

Yet, how different the attitude
to the same task.
Two tots, totally focused on the here and now,
the finding of berries
one at a time
not counting the effort –
just out to munch those berries.

One woman, smiling gently
surprised to find her satisfaction
in the trust of the moment,
the ease and peace
of children picking berries.

Rainbows

I

Rainbows, instantaneous, illusive
Arches connecting heaven and earth
Covenant made visible, vibrant, inclusive
Affirm God's faith in human worth

II

Rainbows sliced in segments
Making light of the promise of care
Their beauty remade, hand-crafted
Helium balloons floating in air

III

Rainbows chopped in fragments
Streamers and shapes gone awry
Jerking strings, pulled by airy whimsies
Joyful, jumping kites against the sky

IV

Rainbows dancing on walls
Playful spirits, flighty and bright
Sunlight caught by crystal balls
Nature's agent frisking light

V

Rainbows hues caught stark and true
Echoing "Let there be Light"
Shapes and contours unmasked through
The lens of a crystal paperweight

COMPANIONS

What started as a solitary walk
was not so solitary after all,
for while I had not sought company
two spirits came to share my path
named Wind and Rain.
And what company they were!

They asked for nothing, only shared:
They shared their strength to pit my strength against.
They shared their play to stimulate my joy.
They shared their energy so I could feel my own.

I'm glad my solitary walk
was not so solitary after all.

Haiku

Bleached moon, mist veil
Consuming calmness, paddling
Towards swelling light

Twin tissue moons, mist
Absorbing stillness, paddling
Towards breaking day

Grey sky, hiding sun
Dripping raindrops on my head
Seasonal pleasure

Barberry bush, quite naked
Borrowing leaves from the maple
Fall's roguish caper

Fine stitches, small beads
Form sunflower mandala
fine art manifest

Blessed Day

For the warmth of the morning sun,
coolness of breezes,
storms coming off the Bay,
salty smell of wetted rocks,
pungent odours of the marsh,
sweet fragrance of firs and spruce
showing off new green fingertips
(as proud as girls with their first manicure),
bunchberries, starflowers, and frivolous violets;
for scampering squirrels,
seals on the Heron Trail and herons on the Seal's
(which shows that native creatures don't
read nor mind our designations), and
ducks and cormorants of course…

for all this
I am thankful and feel the blessing of the day.

I Wonder

I wonder what message, if any, this day
tried to convey in all the things that did not go my way.
The parking meter took my money
but did not give me time.
The concert was moved to a schedule
meddling with my dentist's session.
The extra miles I had to drive
to be in Rothesay twice,
within a short span of time
between the two events –
the dentist and the debate on Paganism.

All the things I want to do, to see, to hear, to learn,
and have to take when offered,
need juggling with needed things,
crowding the time I have available.
Do I try too much? Want too much?
Do I have to make fewer choices?
No, not at all! In spite of all these little irritations,
and sorry to have missed the music, I still had a great day!

Sleigh Ride

Tinkling bells and clopping horse feet
break the silence of the woods.
Our voices, muffled by scarves and other winter gear,
sound like murmurs from afar.
A cold, clear sky with cheery stars so near
it looks as if one could hook
a kite over them with ease, bewitch the view above.

Coming to the camp, deep in the woods,
heat in the hut hits my face at once
yet not reaching my cold feet,
thus sending me scrambling back out
to breath the crisp clean air and share the camaraderie
of friends cooking sausages and chops,
hot chocolate and sweet buns;
sharing steaming tea from the black kettle
hanging over a fire
so large it was not dampened by the dripping
chunks of snow roasting on a stick
held by a child's mittened hands.

Two sleigh trips were needed to convey us all to
this magical setting for fire, food and friendships.
Going back to our cars, some of us prefer to walk
- ice grippers underfoot and, for me, ski poles at the ready -
to end a perfect evening.

Petrified Forest

I feel so inconsequential, so small, so finite
In this vast expanse of sky and land,
Yet, also know that all would not be as is
Without my being here,
An integral part of this infinite, awesome expanse of love,
Its human input blending as natural as that of other life;
Timeless, yet acute, structured in its formlessness,
A place where God rests on the seventh day.

Northern Arizona
March 1994

Security

From above - and below

From left - and right

They guard my secrets, poured out on paper

Non-judgmental, silent

Through the window they watch my struggle to create

Give shape to thoughts, dreams, myself

These branches of elm, locust, spruce

Sentinels of my home, my hideout, my truth.

Three Roses

Three roses, gift from Karen;
three roses for me -
one for Hendrien,
one for mother,
one for oma.

Three in one,
each completing me.
First, the gift of life,
then the grace of motherhood, and now
the bonus blessing of re-generation
all in a gift of love.

Three Roses

Signs of Spring

I

Daffodil trumpets

Speak the unspeakable word

Flowers of hope

II

The snow is going

Now is the time to walk outside -

liberation!

III

Snow boots discarded

Harbour Passage possible

Spring has come in time

IV

I am glad for seasons

They give variety and spice

In my later years

Lilacs

I bought a bunch of lilacs
At the market yesterday.
Feasting on a blossom,
A butterfly, a bonus,
Enlivening the flower
With movement and colour,
Enriching my purchase,
My mood, my room, my life,
With that extra touch.

Notes

Front Door, page 4: In ancient Roman religion and myth, **Janus** is the god of beginnings and transitions thence also of gates, doors, passages, endings and time. He is usually depicted as having two faces, since he looks to the future and to the past. The Romans named the month of January (Ianuarius) in his honour.

Parlor, page 5: The first electricity generating stations in the Saint John area were water powered. Electrical service was thus referred to as "**hydro**."

Dining Room, page 6: "**Old King Cole**" was a commonly served black tea.

Wood Stove, page 10: In ancient Greek religion, **Hestia** is the goddess of the hearth and the right ordering of domesticity.

Master Bedroom, page 13: In classic Greek mythology, **Artemis** is the Hellenic goddess of animals, wilderness, and childbirth.

Back Hall, page 14: In ancient Greek religion and myth, **Demeter** is the goddess of the harvest.

City Bits, page 19: "**Irving bust**" refers to a statue of prominent New Brunswick industrialist, K. C. Irving.

Last Survivor, page 51: "**Dylan-like**" is a reference to the famous poem by Dylan Thomas that begins. "Do not go gentle into that good night, / Old age should burn and rave at close of day; / Rage, rage against the dying of the light."

Groningen 1937, page 62: An "**oude klomp**" is an old wooden shoe.

Herfte, the Netherlands, May 10, 1940, page 65: "**misbegotten Moffen**" refers to Germans.

Walking History Lesson on the Way to School, page 68: "**Quisling**" refers to a person who collaborates with an enemy occupying force. It derives from the name of the Norwegian leader, Vidkun Quisling, who collaborated with the German occupation during the Second World War.

Walking History Lesson on the Way to School, page 68: "… **this old Hansa town**" refers to a town that was part of the Hanseatic League, a 13th-17th century alliance of European trading cities.

Look at This; Do You Remember?, page 74: Somebody sent me a photograph of the house I called home during 1940-1944 when I was 12 –16 years old.

Shifting Rank, page 97: "**opoe**" is grandmother.

Theodorus van Gogh, page 100: Theodorus van Gogh gave two sons the same name, **Vincent Willem**. One died, one survived and became the artist. "**…brother Theo;**" See the book *Dear Theo: The Autobiography of Vincent van Gogh* composed from letters to his brother.

This is My Charlotte, page 102: This poem was written for Charlotte Ritter, a dear friend from Camden, Maine and sent to her with the following note shortly before she died.

> *Dear Charlotte,*
> *Hope this will put a smile on your face… Keep eating those healthy foods. Much love, I am holding you in the Light.*

William Prouty, page 103: Professor of English at University of New Brunswick Saint John, creative writing mentor and convenor of the Purple Wednesday Society, to which this tribute refers.

Rainbows, page 117: The last stanza was inspired by a section of photographs presented by Freeman Patterson's slide show at Kennebecasis Valley High School, Quispamsis, October 22, 1993.

Haiku, page 119: The first two haiku were written during an early morning paddle with Charlotte Ritter on Green Hill Lake during a Quaker weekend gathering, October 13, 2003.

About the Publisher

Chapel Street Editions publishes fine books on the natural history, human history, and cultural life of the Saint John River Region.

We are dedicated to publishing the work of writers and artists of our region, and to publishing books that advance an understanding of the relationship between the natural world, culture, and human adaptation to the environment.

We believe a vibrant cultural life rests on a strong attachment to place: This means a strong attachment to the land, the built environment, and the communities where we live.

For additional information visit
www.chapelstreeteditions.com

www.ingramcontent.com/pod-product-compliance
Ingram Content Group UK Ltd.
Pitfield, Milton Keynes, MK11 3LW, UK
UKHW041639190726
13854UKWH00006B/2581